THE DREAM

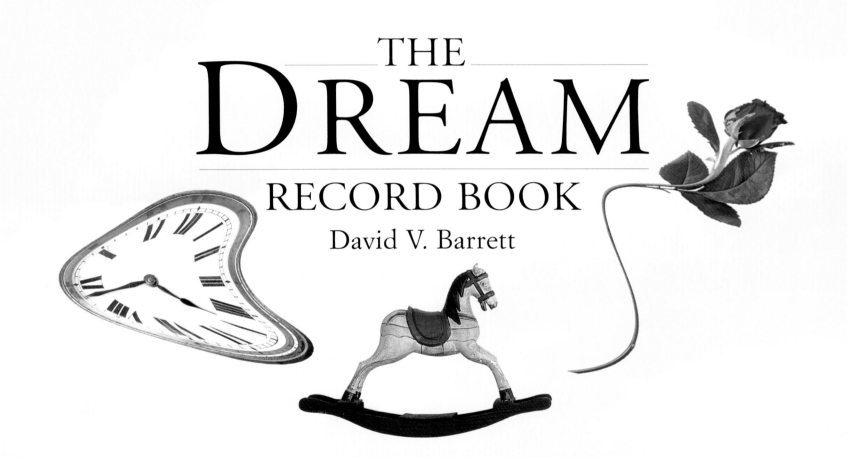

RECORD BOOK

David V. Barrett

DK PUBLISHING, INC.

DK

A DK PUBLISHING BOOK

Design Bernard Higton
Text David V. Barrett
Editor Jacky Jackson

Senior Managing Editor Krystyna Mayer
Managing Editor Jemima Dunne
Managing Art Editor Philip Gilderdale
Senior Art Editor Karen Ward
Production Controller Antony Heller
US Editor Laaren Brown

First published in the United States by
DK Publishing, Inc.
95 Madison Avenue, New York, New York 10016

Visit us on the World Wide Web at
http://www.dk.com

ISBN 0-7894-2075-9

Color reproduction by Mullis Morgan, London
Printed and bound in Singapore by Tien Wah Press Pte. Ltd.

CONTENTS

INTRODUCTION

Some people believe that dreams are messages from the gods, or from the spirit world, and that dreams can foretell the future. This may sometimes be the case, but in *The Dream Record Book* the emphasis is on what dreams can tell you about yourself. There is nothing occult or mystical about this. Our unconscious minds are often aware of aspects of our personalities, or problems in our lives, which our conscious minds do not see or prefer not to acknowledge. We may be able to lie to ourselves about ourselves, but our dreams are more likely to be accurate or truthful – sometimes uncomfortably so.

TYPES OF DREAM

Does this mean, therefore, that every dream is a message from our unconscious to which we must pay careful attention? Almost certainly not. Some dreams appear to be simply replays of some of the day's events, or an anticipation of the next day. To dream of a scene in a film you have just watched, or of a journey the night before you go on vacation, for example, is hardly unusual, and unlikely to be particularly revealing.

Other dreams are just like our waking fantasies, and might be wish-fulfillment – a kind of day-dreaming in our sleep. Likewise in erotic dreams, we are fantasizing about a sexual relationship, often with someone we know and like in our waking life, or sometimes with a well-known personality. Such dreams are probably only significant when the subject of our dream desires is someone completely unexpected, in which case they might well be worth further investigation.

HOW DREAMS CAN HELP

Many dreams are about our fears and insecurities, particularly those which in real life we would not admit to, even to ourselves. In our dreams, our unconscious minds might be pointing out problems and worries that it would be better for us to acknowledge, rather than to ignore. Such dreams can often be very persistent because they meet resistance from the conscious mind. If you have many dreams of this sort, do not worry: so does everyone else. Even the most socially confident, successful, and well-adjusted people have secret doubts about their attractiveness or their abilities. This book can help you to recognize such worries, and to deal with them in your waking life.

READING THE MESSAGE

Is the message in your dream encouraging or warning you? When interpreting your dreams, it is necessary to establish in which direction the message is pointing. For example, if you dream that you are the center of attention at a party, is your dream telling you to have more self-confidence, and that you can be like your dream self? Or is it saying that there is a danger that you are becoming too arrogant and brash in such situations, that you should perhaps calm down a little, and step out of the limelight? The setting, mood, and characters in your dream

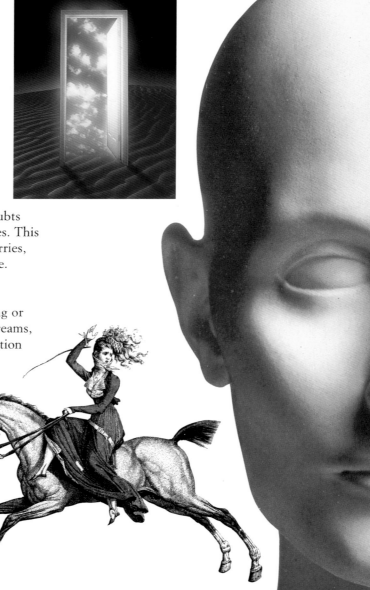

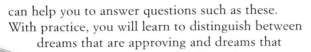

can help you to answer questions such as these. With practice, you will learn to distinguish between dreams that are approving and dreams that are reproving; between those that are encouraging you and those that appear to have a restraining message.

INTEGRATING THE PERSONALITY

In several places in this book the idea of balance is mentioned. Our personalities are not simple or straightforward. We all possess a number of often highly conflicting facets; for example, we all have a mixture of strictness and laxity, of dominance and compliance, of intolerance and tolerance. Dreams can be particularly useful in helping us to identify these different facets within ourselves – each of which is important – and to find out if any one of them is overpowering another. This is why the stories and characters in our dreams often seem outlandish: they are demonstrating in a dramatic way that our personalities or lives are out of balance. Once we learn to identify this sort of message in our dreams, we can begin to do something about it in our waking lives. This is one of the most valuable results of interpreting our dreams.

INDIVIDUAL INTERPRETATION

The most important factor in learning to understand dreams is that they are *your* dreams and, while other people can guide and help, it is up to you to interpret them. Exactly the same dream can mean entirely different things to different people. For this reason, this book is more of a guide book than a dictionary of dream symbols. The book suggests various possible broad meanings for certain general subjects that frequently occur in dreams, and asks, "What does this mean to you?" Analysts such as Sigmund Freud, Carl Jung, and others have provided many general meanings of dream symbols, and these can be helpful – but in the final analysis, only you can say what a particular symbol in your dream means to you. Within the framework of suggestions given in this book, you should follow your own instincts when interpreting your dreams, and build up your own individual guide to your dreams.

USING THIS BOOK

Finally, this is a book that you are intended to write in; there is an explanation of the best way to do this in Recording Your Dreams (*see p. 28*). Once you begin to record your dreams, you will find that this is the start of an exciting voyage of discovery. At first it might seem difficult to remember your dreams, let alone interpret them; but remember, it does become easier with practice. The further you progress with the study of your own dreams, the more fascinating and fulfilling you will find the exercise.

You will certainly discover that the more often you record your dreams the more you will remember them. You may notice repeating patterns of subjects and characters, in addition to the recurrent dreams that you may already be familiar with. You may even learn to alter the course of your dreams sometimes; in several places in this book it is suggested that you try to do this to gain further understanding of the deeper meanings of your dreams, and to learn to control and change the less pleasant aspects. Most important of all, as you grow practiced in interpreting your dreams, you will discover much more about yourself, and this will help you to improve your waking life.

PART ONE

DREAM THEMES

THIS SECTION examines many of the most frequent and important themes that occur in dreams. It looks at the people or animals that might appear in your dreams, the significance of any dominant mood, color, or emotion of a dream, and the meanings of dream images such as buildings, or structures. It also suggests what dreams of movement, energy, and creativity might tell you about yourself in real life, and explains the appearance of religious and mythological figures in your dreams.

Use this first section to help you work out what these themes might mean within the context of your dreams. Make a note of your own dreams on the relevant pages, and see how your personal library of dream themes builds up alongside your dream interpretations in the second part of this book. Remember to cross-reference your notes in both parts of the book.

As you explore these themes you will become familiar with their occurrence in your dreams, and will come to understand them more clearly.

HUMAN LIFE

YOU MAY ACTUALLY KNOW the people in your dreams, or they may be complete strangers, or even famous personalities. People you know in real life may appear as themselves or sometimes, as Carl Jung believed (*see p. 34*), they may take on archetypal roles; for example, when a friend appears as a typical authority figure, say in a priest's robes, you may feel the need to ask this person for spiritual advice. The people in your dreams can often represent different aspects of your own personality, so ask yourself how they are behaving and how you feel about them.

If two people are arguing in your dream, this may reflect an inner struggle between your cautious side, say, and your adventurous side, or your forbidden desires battling against your need to appear respectable. Always listen carefully to both sides of the argument, because they both come from within you. Your unconscious may be aware of this conflict in your personality and this is why it surfaces in your dreams.

AUTHORITY FIGURES
Sometimes the people in your dreams appear as authority figures – teacher, policeman, judge, even your own father. Although they might be the "voice" of your guilty conscience, more often they are there to guide and instruct rather than to chastise. Note what they do and say, and write it down as soon as you wake up, because often they have important messages from your wiser inner self.

If you are wearing a uniform, this could show your attitude to conformity. Your dream might be showing that you fear or dislike conforming to society's rules, or that you are too willing to conform without thinking for yourself. If your uniform is neat and precise, this might be a comment on how you project yourself in real life; if it is torn and dirty, this could be an indication of your concern about how other people see you. If you are the only one not in uniform, do you see yourself as a rebel?

FAMILY RELATIONSHIPS
Dreaming of your family can suggest caring for others, or the need for love, emotional warmth, and stability. If you are a child in the dream, there may be a message of dependence; if you are an adult with children, there may be a message that responsibility is needed. Dreaming of a birth or death might represent the beginning or end of something important in life, such as a job, a project, or a relationship.

HAIR
This dream symbol can be interpreted in many ways, depending partly on your personal preferences, partly on the fashionable norms, and partly on your deep cultural beliefs. If your hair seems significant in the dream, there are several possibilities to consider. While long, flowing hair can suggest freedom from restriction, it might also denote sensuality or, for a male dreamer, rebellion. For a man, having all your hair cut off could reveal a fear of loss of power in your daily life, or it could be a fear of the loss of your virility. For a woman, having your hair cut off could represent sacrifice, like a nun, or shame, like a prisoner. In general, dreams about losing your hair suggest that there is some major insecurity in your life. What is it that is worrying you so much?

EATING AND DRINKING
In a dream, what you take into your body becomes a part of you – much in the way a primitive warrior believed that eating the heart of a brave opponent would add to his strength. What are you eating – are you taking in good food at a rich banquet, or

are you eating "junk" food? This can be telling you that you are filling your life with worthwhile or worthless activities. The preparation of food suggests your care and love for others. Feeling hunger might reveal a lack in your life – is there something that you really need?

NAKEDNESS

The appearance in your dreams of naked people, or your own nakedness, is a fairly common yet complex dream symbol. It is important to consider your mood during the dream – are you feeling anxious, or relaxed, or sensual? If you are the only clothed person in the dream, perhaps in your waking life you conceal too much of yourself from others. If you are the only person who is naked, perhaps you want to be the center of attention; maybe you are too open about yourself to others, and this dream is showing your fear of vulnerability.

Nakedness is linked with sexuality and, depending on the mood of the dream, it could be telling you something about feelings of shame, or perhaps revealing a fear of sexual inadequacy. On the other hand, a dream of nakedness could also reveal a desire to return to the innocence of childhood.

A RECORD OF YOUR DREAMS ABOUT HUMAN LIFE

IMAGE	HOW IT APPEARED	DREAM NO. IN DIARY

MOOD AND EMOTIONS

THE MOOD OF A DREAM is perhaps the most important single indicator of its significance. If you dream of being with or talking to someone you know, for instance, the dream will have a different message if throughout it you are feeling apprehensive, angry, or ashamed, rather than peaceful, excited, or loving.

Sometimes when we wake from a dream it is only the mood that remains; the story, characters, and setting have faded, and all we can recall is a strong feeling of sadness, fear, or joy, which can sometimes linger for hours. It is worth recording these moods, perhaps in a notebook, to see if there is a pattern to your emotions.

WHAT ARE YOUR EMOTIONS TELLING YOU?
Sometimes the mood is closely linked to the story of the dream, and reinforces whatever the dream is about. On other occasions, the mood might be completely at variance with the situation in the

dream, and here you need to pay more attention. Why, in a dream about a walk with a friend, do you feel nervous? Why, when you dream about stepping into a boxing ring to face the world heavyweight champion, do you feel relaxed and confident? Making a note of the mood, the people, the place, and the action will help you to work out why you felt a particular emotion in a particular situation. Perhaps the dream about walking with your friend is telling you to be wary of someone you thought was reliable. Perhaps your dream about boxing is telling you that you are stronger than you thought. Always examine the mood closely, because it is the mood that very often holds the key to interpreting the dream.

REMEMBERING THE MOOD
Try to remember the mood of each dream rather than your reaction to the subject matter. If, for example, you dream of a close friend or a member of your family who has died, you might wake up remembering the event and feel sad. But this could be your waking reaction to the loss. In your dream the person might have been alive and well; by reminding you of this, your unconscious mind is bringing you a message of hope or encouragement. So reach back into the dream and try to recapture the mood that was actually there; if it was a happy, positive mood, this could help you to come to terms with your loss. Your dreams are more likely to be helpful than hurtful or distressing if you approach them in the right way.

VIOLENT DREAMS
It is upsetting if you have a dream in which you or someone else is violent or even murderous, yet this could be a safety valve, a way of letting off steam and releasing tensions that you feel in real life. After all, when someone has annoyed you, it is obviously better to kill them in a dream than in reality. If you frequently have such violent dreams, you should first look for clues for the reasons within the dreams, then at your life.

EROTIC DREAMS
These often carry a strong emotional charge because they are not always simply fantasy wish-fulfillment; they can be suggesting, through the intrusive feelings of guilt or anxiety, that you look more closely at how a current relationship is working, what you are bringing to it, and what you are getting out of it.

SYMBOLS OF EMOTION

In certain dreams, your mood is disguised within some other image or symbol. Here are a few topics that might be indicators of the emotional message of a dream.

Aggressive Combat

For obvious reasons, weapons of any kind usually imply aggression. If you dream of shooting someone or running a sword through them, this could indicate feelings of sexual aggression, anger, or frustration. If your dreams are warning you of this tendency, pay attention to the warning. Weapons used in a competition might suggest that a more mental battle is going on in your life. Is a real-life relationship so combative that your dream is warning you that someone might get hurt?

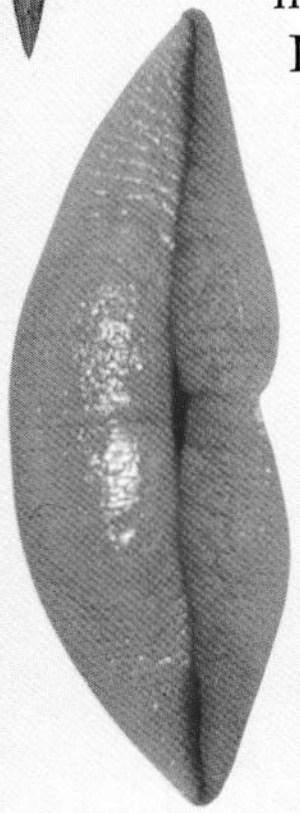

Moods as Colors

Colors (*see p. 20*) can be a clear indication of a dream's mood. Red could suggest passion or anger; blue is generally considered peaceful, but it can also imply sexual frigidity or a blocking of any emotional reaction. A dominance of dark colors might suggest a heavy mood or a sense of oppression.

Weather Warnings

A dream of stormy weather could indicate that you are experiencing a storm of violent emotions. A dull, gray day could imply a dismal or depressed mood. Warm, sunny weather usually indicates a happy mood, but stuffy, humid weather might suggest that you feel oppressed or claustrophobic.

A RECORD OF THE MOODS AND EMOTIONS IN YOUR DREAMS

MOOD/EMOTION	HOW IT AFFECTED YOUR DREAM	DREAM NO. IN DIARY

MOVEMENT

VERY FEW DREAMS are simple, static pictures; usually, as in life or even in films, you or the dream's characters move around and interact with each other. Although this dream activity or interaction seems normal, it can be important in itself because it can reveal how you communicate with others.

Most people have dreams of running, falling, flying, or swimming, of chasing or being chased, of driving a car or being a passenger. All of these can carry significant messages and, if they recur, you may find that you can gain a degree of control if you try some of the suggestions given here.

FALLING

This is a very common dream theme, which usually implies that you feel out of control and helpless or fearful in your real life. Did you jump, or were you pushed? Are you desperately trying to escape from a feeling of shame or despair, or do you feel that you have failed someone? As you fall, look around you and see where you are falling from, and to. See if there is something you can catch hold of to break your fall, or try to remember that you have a parachute you can open to save yourself. Try to control your landing, and if you land, take note of whether it is a hard landing, which could be a warning to take care, or a soft landing, in which case your fears may not be as devastating as you imagined.

FLYING

Although Sigmund Freud (*see p. 32*) saw flying dreams as sexual, and indeed some may well be, others signify that you desire freedom or liberation, or to cast off the problems and ties of the world below you. Whether you are like a bird, soaring and diving at will, or piloting an airplane, with responsibility for others, or even a passenger, with no control over the flight, all these elements will tell you something about how you feel about your journey through life.

BEING PURSUED

This extremely common dream theme often recurs, and can be quite disturbing. When it next happens, try to analyze each part of it. Do you know who is chasing you? Is it an actual person, perhaps someone who you feel is overtaking you at work? Or are you being pursued by your lover? Maybe your pursuer is not a person at all but a formless fear, even some aspect of your personality. In this case, instead of running away, turn to face your

fear and identify it, simply asking, "Who are you? Why are you chasing me?" If you face your fear, and can identify the problem in your real life, you are more likely to be able to deal with the problem.

SWIMMING

Water is symbolic of the emotions and of the spiritual life; if you are swimming in your dream, this could be an indication of your inner or emotional well-being. Are you in the middle of a vast ocean, or being carried along in a fast-running river, or trapped in a small, stagnant pond? If you are swimming strongly and confidently toward an attainable goal, this is a positive sign indicating that you are happy with where you are going. If there is no shore in sight, and you are beginning to tire, try to relax, lie back in the water and let it support you; your sea of emotion is very strong.

DRIVING

Driving fast is a well-known Freudian image of sexual power, particularly for male dreamers, but it can also point to the enjoyment of any power for male or female dreamers. It may signify a desire for success, or an unconscious recognition that sex or the desire for power may be the driving force in your life – especially if the car seems out of control. If the car crashes or breaks down, it is likely that you have strong fears of weakness or inadequacy.

If you dream about driving in a town, or out in the countryside, pay attention to what you see, and to who is in the car with you. While this could be a dream of normal domestic activity, it may also suggest that, since you are in the driving seat (and in control of your own life), there are areas of your life you need to explore in more detail.

GOING THROUGH A TUNNEL

This has a very obvious sexual connotation, which should always be considered in the interpretation – but it may also have a wider meaning. The tunnel may represent the journey we all make through life, or perhaps a journey of discovery that you need to make into your own unconscious. A tunnel is usually dark, and sometimes scary; perhaps you need to pass through a period of darkness to reach the light. Are you in a car or on a train or walking through the tunnel? The car or train may be reminding you that you are not alone. If you are alone, this could indicate a real-life situation you must work through on your own. Note where the tunnel began, and where it ends; these may be important clues to where you feel you have got to in your life so far.

BEING TRAPPED

If in your dream you cannot move, or your movements are constricted, it could simply be that you are caught in the bedclothes. Or it could be a sign that in real life you feel trapped in a situation in which there are few options open to you. Look around in your dream for a direction in which you can move, and then see what this might suggest about your situation in life.

A RECORD OF YOUR DREAMS ABOUT MOVEMENT

IMAGE	HOW IT APPEARED	DREAM NO. IN DIARY

ENERGY AND CREATIVITY

THERE ARE TIMES when you wake from a dream astonished – and sometimes exhausted – by all the activity within it. For what seemed hours you might have been dancing, taking part in sports, or even building a cathedral out of matchsticks. Sometimes these physical or mental activities are things you do in real life, but often they are not. Why does your unconscious put so much effort into them? What is this telling you?

There are probably several answers: if you devote most of your daily life to serious work, maybe your mind is taking the opportunity to play for a while; or perhaps it is suggesting that you should take up a hobby. If your life is sedentary, dreaming of sports may be a hint that you need to take up some form of physical activity. When your dreams put you in an unfamiliar situation where you have to use your strength, skill, or wits to solve a problem, they might be showing you by analogy how to solve a problem in your real life.

MUSIC
Whether you can play an instrument in real life or not, you may find yourself playing or listening to music in your dream. Music is one of the most powerful creative forces, and although melody, harmony, and rhythm are all important in music-playing, they can also be metaphors for aspects of your life. If you are playing in a group or an orchestra, are you in tune and in step with the others, or are you creating disharmony? Sometimes the name of the music is a clue to something else

entirely – it could be significant by association, perhaps to a person, an episode, or a place that has meant a great deal to you in the past or that you should now pay attention to.

PAINTING OR DRAWING
Although Freud saw pens, pencils, and paint-brushes as phallic symbols, it is worth looking at other meanings. Are you drawing or painting something that you need to examine more closely in real life? Or are you trying, for good or for bad, to create your own version of reality? Perhaps your dream is suggesting that you should draw or paint, as well as write down your dreams; this can often be a valuable interpretative exercise.

MODEL-MAKING OR SCULPTING
Look closely at what you are making in your dream. Does the model or sculpture represent someone or something in your real life? It may be suggesting that the solution to a difficulty lies in reducing it to manageable proportions. Or perhaps it reflects your hidden desire to be creative about your problems.

WRITING
If you are writing a letter, to whom is it addressed, and what does it say? Perhaps in real life you should contact that person? If you are writing an article, a story, or a book, is its content relevant to anything in your real life? All writing is a form of communication; perhaps your dream is saying that you should be in touch more with others. Writing that is full of blots and cross-outs could indicate the need to take more care when communicating. Try to read what is being written; it could be an unadorned message from your unconscious.

ACTING

We play many roles in our waking lives. At any one time we can be either friend, lover, parent, child, spouse, teacher, student, and many other things – sometimes we can be several at the same time. In our dreams, these different roles are often acted out individually by different characters. Such dreams can be very illuminating; by looking at them closely we can begin to understand the complexities of our own personalities.

When, in your dream, you find yourself on a stage or being filmed, this can be very significant. Drama is, after all, a way of representing life. Look at the storyline: does it have any relevance to your waking life? You could be acting out a problematic real-life situation: see what you can learn from this "replay." A dream about acting can tell you much about how you see yourself – are you the center of attention, and is the spotlight on you? If so, do you want to be so highly visible, or are you scared? Perhaps your dream is saying that you put yourself forward too much? If you feel you are just a minor character, of no real importance, it may mean that you need to take on a more major role in your life.

If you have stage fright in the dream, or forget your lines, this could be a comment on your lack of confidence, or on problems you may be having with communication. Feeling that you are under the control of the director or scriptwriter could suggest that all your moves in real life are being dictated or directed by others. Or perhaps your dream is really telling you that you are acting or pretending about some particular aspect of your life. You might also consider if you are making a drama out of a minor problem or difficulty you have encountered.

A RECORD OF YOUR DREAMS ABOUT ENERGY AND CREATIVITY

IMAGE	HOW IT APPEARED	DREAM NO. IN DIARY

THE NATURAL WORLD

WAKING UP in a strange place, people often ask, "Where am I?" You should ask yourself the same question about your dreams. The place where you find yourself is the setting for your dream, and can be as significant as anything else in it. The kind of landscape reveals where your inner self is situated, while weather conditions such as wind and rain can reflect your mood.

Dreams often draw on traditional, deep-seated beliefs. Until recently, for example, it was believed that everything in life (including

people) was made up of the four "elements": Earth was seen as relating to material, worldly matters; Air denoted the intellect, thought, and communication; Fire represented energy, passion, and creativity; and Water had to do with the emotions, the spiritual life, and sensitivity.

MOUNTAIN OR HILL

If you are on or approaching a high mountain, this could represent a reaching up into the heavens or the spiritual world; perhaps you need to focus on exploring this part of your life. If you are climbing a mountain, this usually means that you are making a great effort to achieve the summit, which may relate to some goal in your waking life. In Freudian terms, a mountain peak thrusting into the sky can be seen as a phallic symbol, and may represent your sexual desires. Gently rounded hills are more suggestive of female breasts, and wandering in such hills could indicate sexual exploration.

VALLEY

If you are entering a peaceful valley or cleft between two gently rounded hills, this is possibly a sexual image. Allow its message of peacefulness into your waking sex life. If the dream's overall tone is despondent, however, and the valley you enter is dark and gloomy, this may indicate that you need to pass through a dark time before you can come out on the other side. While in this valley, look around to see if there is anything to indicate the purpose of your visit: are you on a journey, for example, or simply taking exercise?

VOLCANO

Whether erupting or dormant, a volcano can simply represent masculine potency, but it might also represent the force of explosive anger. Does this worry you in your dream? Rather than giving a warning about getting too angry, dreaming about a volcano could indicate that you need to release your pent-up anger and frustrations before you get to the explosive stage.

SEA, LAKE, POOL, OR RIVER

Water, which represents your emotions, is one of the most important of all dream symbols. Since your unconscious mind is far more in touch with your emotions than is your conscious mind, your dreams can hold many important messages for you.

What kind of water is in your dream? A sea or a lake represents the great sea of the emotions: note whether it is storm-tossed, or tranquil, or even completely flat. How do you feel about the water? If you are struggling, or feel that you are drowning, what emotional problem is on your mind? If you are standing on a shore, are you enjoying the nearness of the sea, or does it frighten you? This may show that you fear involvement – getting immersed – in your emotions. Being on a boat can represent the journey of your life. How is the voyage going? Are you lost, or do you know where you are going?

If you are looking at a pool, whether it is clear and clean, or murky and stagnant, can tell you much about your own emotional state. Likewise, a river that flows – boiling fast or tepidly slow – is telling you what your emotions are really like.

CLIMATE

This can be an indicator of your present mood; is it sunny, cloudy, calm, or stormy? Rain is not always negative – it is life-giving and perhaps represents spiritual refreshment from above. The feeling of heat in dreams is sensual as long as it is enjoyable; a burning desert might indicate that your life is arid.

TREES AND FLOWERS

A tree might represent natural growth, the goodness of nature, strength, and stability. Trees are revered in many old religions, so if the tree's branches reach up to the sky, it could symbolize spiritual growth. If you are watching a tree growing, this could be reference to the development of maturity.

Dreams about flowers suggest a natural, healthy life and, often, sexuality. Some flowers have specific meanings: daffodils, for instance, are usually a sign of spring, with all the promise that implies. The rose is the most significant of flowers; depending on other factors in your dream, a rose can symbolize secrecy and spirituality, as well as virginity or female sexuality.

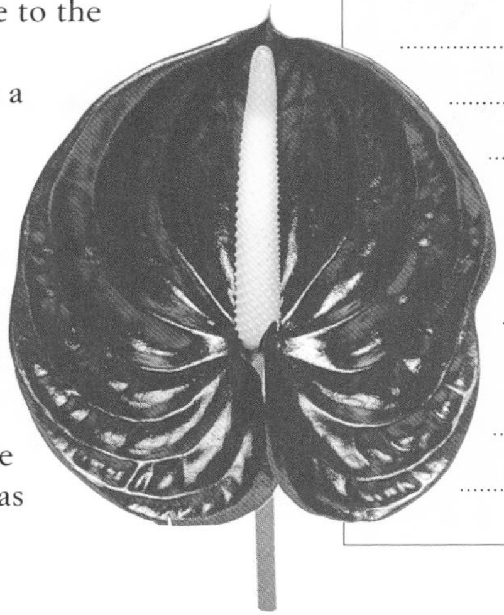

A RECORD OF YOUR DREAMS ABOUT THE NATURAL WORLD

IMAGE	HOW IT APPEARED	DREAM NO. IN DIARY

The Animal World

ANIMALS OF ALL KINDS, big or small, can be among the most fascinating aspects of your dreams. Familiar animals such as your own cat or dog, or cows and sheep in the country, or pigeons in a town square may behave normally in your dream. They may also behave in unusual ways by speaking to you, or guiding you, in which case you should listen carefully to what they have to say.

Sometimes animals simply represent themselves; at other times they can represent people you know (you can probably think of someone who is as gentle as a lamb, or as wise as an owl), and sometimes they represent aspects of your own personality. Animals feature prominently in our everyday language in the form of proverbs or figures of speech; dreams often make use of these, so keep them in mind when you analyze your dreams. Although the attributes of animals have different meanings in various cultures, consider the traditional attributes of the animal, as well as what it means to you personally.

BIRDS
In general, birds represent freedom of movement, the spirit soaring into the sky, the aiming for and perhaps achievement of high ambitions. Try to identify the type of bird; a predatory hawk or a peaceful dove clearly symbolize different things.

An eagle, for instance, is the master of the air. From its great height it can survey the land and its prey beneath. If you dream that you are an eagle, do you feel superior to everyone? If an eagle is flying with you, note where it takes you, and what it shows you.

A caged bird suggests imprisonment. Do you feel trapped and confined? Try opening the door of the cage in your dream to gain your freedom. Perhaps this caged bird symbolizes something in your life that is very beautiful, but that you are keeping locked up. Perhaps you feel that you are unable to spread your wings and perform to your full potential in your waking life.

CATS
These are beautiful, sleek, and sensual animals, but can you really trust them? Independent and willful, they are also excellent predators. Could the cat in your dream represent someone you know? Perhaps you are aware of a cat's attributes in yourself, or your dream could be telling you that you need to be more sensual, or more independent.

DOGS
A dog is often seen as a loyal, faithful friend, a good companion along life's way, but consider the sort of dog you dreamed about – was it a fierce guard dog, a hunting dog, a sheepdog, a small lap dog? How did you feel about the dog? Do you

know anyone the dog could represent? Or is the dog really yourself? Analyze your dream to find out whether any of the dog's attributes are too weak or too strong in your own personality.

FARM ANIMALS
These animals are providers of food, clothing, or a service to humankind. A cow represents nourishment, because of its milk, and safe, warm, maternal domesticity. A bull represents masculine power or uncontrolled anger. Sheep follow without much thought; are you perhaps mindlessly following fashions, or social, political, or religious beliefs, without thinking them through for yourself? Look at what these animals mean to you.

PREDATORY OR WILD ANIMALS
Lions and wolves are strong, fierce animals, but there is no need to fear them in your dreams. Lions, who are protective of their families, are traditionally regarded as noble creatures, while wolves live and hunt in packs that have a strong hierarchy. Should you pay attention to any of these attributes in your waking life? Folk stories often contain much useful wisdom about wild animals such as these. Do you know someone who is like a lion or a wolf – and is your dream about that person?

FISHES

Fishes swim effortlessly in water, and water usually represents the emotions and the spiritual side of life in dreams. If a fish is swimming near you, follow it to see where it takes you; you may need guidance in your present emotional situation, and the fish in your dream can be trusted to show you the way.

SNAKES

A snake is a complex dream symbol. Many people have an instinctive fear of snakes. Yet snakes also suggest wisdom, and when coiled around a stick, are a powerful symbol of healing. In the Bible, the snake symbolizes temptation and sexuality. A snake coiled in a circle represents reincarnation.

SPIDERS

Another contradictory dream symbol, spiders are feared and hated by many, yet in Native American culture they suggest creativity, and in Scottish culture, perseverance. Are you trapped in a web in your real life? Or are you sitting at the center of your life, drawing others into your intrigues?

BEES

Known to be hard workers, bees provide honey, and can therefore represent the provision of nourishment and goodness. In certain cultures, a bee is also an ancient symbol of wisdom, and it is customary to tell bees your news.

A RECORD OF YOUR DREAMS ABOUT THE ANIMAL WORLD

IMAGE	HOW IT APPEARED	DREAM NO. IN DIARY

Like a dog, he hunts in dreams

COLORS

IF YOU ARE PARTICULARLY STRUCK by the colors in your dreams, take note of them because dominant colors can have different meanings. Viewing things in a deep red light or a soft blue light, for example, will clearly have a different emotional impact. Often, though, the unusual color of an animal, or the color of the clothes of a major character in your dream, will catch your attention because it is out of the ordinary.

If the scene, person, or animal is in your favorite color, it might be representing you. If there are two clashing colors in the dream, perhaps these denote aspects of your life that are out of harmony with each other.

RED

This is a vibrant, active, traditionally masculine color. Depending on the rest of the dream, red could suggest force, aggression, conflict, or danger. Red can also imply the heat of passion, and because it is the color of fire, it can be seen as dangerous. Red is also the color of warmth or cheerfulness. Depending on its hue, it is the color of blood, and of wine, and so might suggest sacrifice. In certain situations red can mean stop, or a warning. It is a color that demands to be noticed.

BLUE

This is a cool color; a person dressed in blue is likely to have a sensible, thoughtful message for you, which you should listen to carefully. It is the color of intellect and can represent spiritual purity – the Virgin Mary is usually shown dressed in blue – so perhaps there is a spiritual or moral message here. For men, it might be suggesting that they listen to their intuitive, or "feminine," side.

GREEN

Primarily the color of nature and growing things, green is also the color of spring, new beginnings, inexperience, and progress. But it can also, depending on the shade, and obviously on the context, be the color of poison, and so a warning of a hidden threat. In many cultures, green denotes jealousy and envy – ask yourself whether you are envious of anyone in the dream, or they of you.

YELLOW

A bright, cheerful color, the color of the sun, or of life-giving pollen, yellow is often seen as a positive color. In some cultures, however, yellow

means cowardice; is your dream showing that you are running away from something? If it is a sickly yellow, it could suggest illness.

PURPLE

Purple was considered a rare and rich color which, because it was worn by people of rank, such as Roman senators, bishops, and royalty, usually suggests a desire for success, esteem, or high authority in those who wear it.

GOLD

Gold is usually associated with royalty (gold crowns) and with wealth (gold money). If someone in your dream is dressed in gold, do you feel in awe of them? This may be a person of high or noble position – perhaps even a god-like figure, whose instructions you should obey. If there are a lot of gold objects, your dream could be telling you that you are paying too much attention to the accumulation of material things.

SILVER

Because it is seen as the feminine equivalent of gold, silver is associated with goddesses and queens. Like gold, silver can also denote money, jewelry, and wealth. But silver is also the color of the Moon, and so of things that are partly hidden. It can suggest the unconscious and the esoteric. It often denotes inner spirituality, rather than the outer trappings of religion.

ORANGE

A bright, lively color, this is likely to denote positive things such as happiness, health, or inner peace. Saffron is also a spiritual color in some Eastern religions.

BROWN

This is the color of the material or earthly world. Depending on the context, it can represent the soil – a source of good, healthy nourishment. It suggests perhaps that you need to dig deeply into your natural resources for your sustenance – or it could be dirt or mud that is smearing and obscuring your vision, or is bogging you down.

WHITE

This is the color of purity and spirituality, completion, or death. In societies where white is worn at funerals, death is seen as a beginning rather than an end. Seeing things too much in pure white, however, could indicate that you are being blinded to the subtle shades of reality. Perhaps you are neglecting or are unable to see the important details in your life?

BLACK

This is a very somber color – in fact, it is literally the lack of all color and light, and spiritually can mean the absence of God. Ask yourself what is lacking in your real life, or what you are concealing or denying. Are you keeping secrets, even from yourself? A figure dressed in black from head to toe is likely to seem threatening. The appearance of such a figure could signify a dark side to your personality that you need to explore. Or the blackness of your dream could be a warning of depression. If this is so, look for hope in the other colors in this and other dreams.

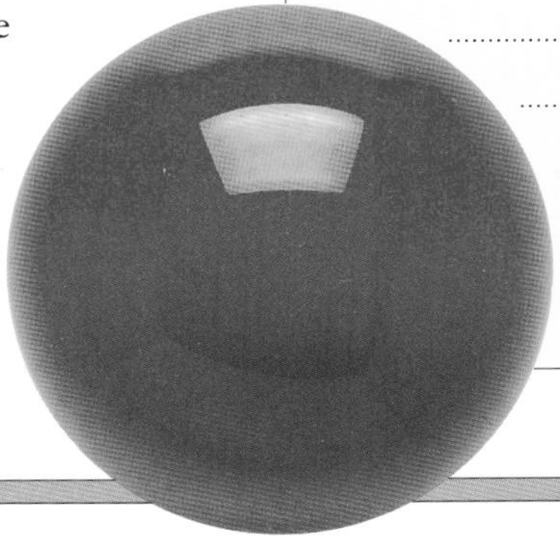

A RECORD OF THE COLORS IN YOUR DREAMS

COLOR	HOW IT APPEARED	DREAM NO. IN DIARY

BUILDINGS AND STRUCTURES

A BUILDING OR STRUCTURE in a dream can be interpreted in several different ways; it may simply be a setting, familiar or not, for the story of the dream, or it may be significant in itself – especially if there is anything unusual about it.

A dream set in a school could be about teaching or learning new ways; one set in a place of worship may be telling you something about your spiritual life. A bar or deli is often the focus of social life, and an office the work environment, indicating organization and

status; a station suggests your zest for or fear of traveling. A bridge that spans difficult terrain can be a link between two places or events. To see if this is a metaphor for two areas in your life that are or should be linked, try to identify what is below the bridge and what is at each end. Were you afraid to cross over, or did you feel that it was the only way to get to where you wanted to go?

HOUSE
In a dream a house usually represents you, the dreamer. Look carefully to see which room you are in, because this is significant. Do you feel at ease

there? If there is someone with you, who are they? Are they invited, or are they intruders? What is the room like? Is it neat or a dirty, dusty mess; is it bare and unwelcoming, or warm and comforting? If you are doing something out of place, such as preparing a meal in the bathroom, your dream may be telling you that you need to integrate aspects of your personality or your waking life.

Particular rooms can represent different aspects of the personality. Although interpretations of the rooms of a house are generally agreed on by dream analysts, there are not hard and fast rules. The following ideas can be used as a starting point in your self-analysis.

Living Room
This room (or your den if you have one) represents the heart of the home, and thus your deepest inner self, the core of your personality. Because it is the focus of sharing and family life, you should feel at ease here. If in your dream you do not, try to work out what is causing you unrest.

Fireplace
No matter which room the fireplace is in, it suggests safety, warmth, companionship, and domesticity.

Attic
This is where your higher consciousness or spiritual aspirations are to be found. It is also the place where you store unwanted objects. If you dream that you are in an attic, what can you see? Why are you there? If you are searching for something, perhaps there is an aspect of your personality or desires that you have hidden away for too long and now want to find again.

Halls, Corridors, and Passages
These can represent female sexuality, and often appear in dreams suggesting sexual security or insecurity. What is the mood of your dream – happy, excited, or fearful?

Bedroom
A bedroom is a place of rest, renewal, and sexual relations. If you dream of conflict here, you need to examine your dream carefully.

Bathroom
This denotes the cleansing of the mind or spirit, or ridding yourself of dross; if you have dreamed of a bathroom, why did you feel the need to do this?

Kitchen
This is a place of practical activity, of sharing work together with a partner or children. If in your dream you are preparing food in the kitchen, is the food fresh, interesting, and appetizing, or is it dull and stale, or even rotting? The kitchen, usually warm and welcoming, is also representative of nurturing and love.

Basement
Here lies the unconscious, or those things dreamers bury deeply. If you look around a basement you may find things you would prefer not to, or things that you hoped you had forgotten. It is important, however, to know what is down there.

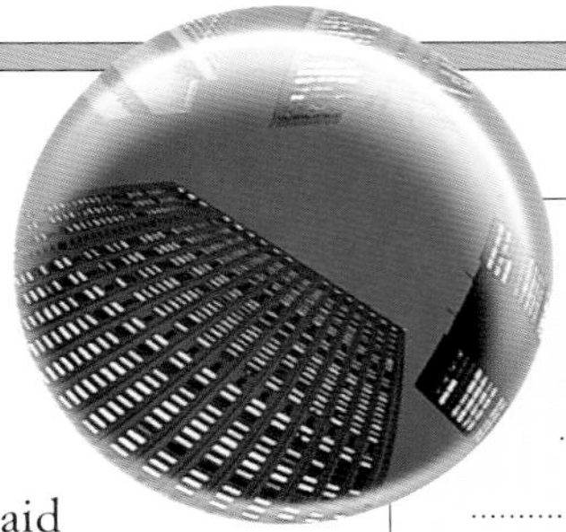

Stairs

These can represent sexual intercourse; they can also suggest that the dreamer is exploring other levels of the personality. Were they steep or easy to climb? Were you afraid that you might fall down them, or did you see them as the best way up?

Walls

Walls can sometimes suggest separation, that the dreamer is cut off from outside reality. Walls can enclose or trap you, or a part of your personality. On the other hand, walls need to be strong enough to hold up the house. If in your dream your outside walls are crumbling, do you feel vulnerable?

Doors

These represent the orifices of the body. The front door of a house may represent the mouth, hence communication. Is the door in your dream open or shut? If you cannot open or close it, why not?

Windows

These are often representative of the eyes, which are called the windows of the soul. If in your dream you are on the inside, looking out, what can you see? Can others see in? Do you want them to? Are the windows open or closed? If they are open, are you letting fresh air in, and is there a clear view in and out? Are the windows clean or dirty? If they are dirty, perhaps you view the outside world through a distorting layer of grime or unhappiness.

Outside of House

This represents the image you show to the world. In your dream, is there a high fence that cuts off all view of your house and your true self? Does your house look untidy and hostile, or clean and friendly? These may all be things that you can respond to.

A RECORD OF YOUR DREAMS ABOUT BUILDING AND STRUCTURES

IMAGE	HOW IT APPEARED	DREAM NO. IN DIARY

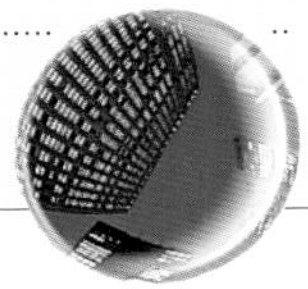

RELIGION AND MYTHOLOGY

THE IMAGERY of religion and mythology plays an important part in everyone's life, and often appears in our dreams. Churches, synagogues, and mosques are part of the architecture we see everywhere, and they can at times be the unlikely settings for our dreams. Religious figures such as old gods, bishops, or rabbis may appear as dream characters. When this occurs, it is likely that your unconscious mind is reminding you about your spiritual or moral life, and using a sacred place or a religious leader to give the message authority.

RELIGIOUS IMAGES
Like religion, dreams use many metaphors. Often these are taken from Bible stories, or from well-known paintings about such stories: Noah and the Ark, Moses and the Ten Commandments, Jesus feeding the Five Thousand. In other instances, the imagery is less well defined but could still have an important spiritual message: two sticks might form a cross; a wine glass might represent a chalice; a halo of light might appear behind someone's head.

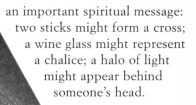

MYTHOLOGY
Even if we have not studied other religions, most of us are aware of them, and of Greek, Roman, and Norse mythology. Sometimes religious figures of the ancient world (or references to them) appear as themselves. We may dream of Odin, the Norse All-Father, with his floppy hat, his one eye, and his two ravens. It is more likely, however, that the figures we dream about are disguised or represented by primordial images or archetypes.

ARCHETYPES
The psychologist Carl Jung (*see p. 34*) found that people of many different religions and cultures seem to draw on much the same group of figures or archetypes in both their mythologies and their dreams. He suggested that each of us has access to a "collective unconscious," a huge pool of images from which our dreams can draw. The following lists some of the most important archetypes that might appear in your dreams – and their meanings. Learn to recognize these archetypes, and be aware of their roles and their messages.

The Naive Seeker or Fool
Often you, the dreamer, might appear as naive or foolish in your dream; you seem to be stepping out immature and unprepared for the journey of life. Remember that this Fool figure, like Perceval in the earliest Grail legends, is also a Seeker after knowledge and experience. If you dream about being naive or foolish, the dream may be suggesting that you have something important to learn.

The Wise Old Man
This figure might appear in your dreams as a king, judge, priest, or teacher, a stern but kindly uncle, or as your own father – in other words, someone from whom you are prepared (or need) to accept perhaps unwelcome words of wisdom, or moral approval or disapproval.

The Earth Mother
She is a similar figure to the Wise Old Man, but with more emphasis on female wisdom. When she appears in your dreams she may have messages about healing and childbirth. She is a mother-goddess figure, loving and nurturing, but quite prepared to give you a slap if you deserve it.

The Magician or Trickster
Occasionally a character in a dream provides an apparently "magical" solution to a problem. This solution might be suggesting that you look at a real-life problem from a different perspective. But be careful: the Magician is also a Trickster, as were the gods Loki and Pan, and the Native North American Coyote figure; any of these archetypes might appear in the role of Magician or Trickster. Sometimes your unconscious plays tricks on you; the Magician is not always to be believed or relied on.

The Anima and Animus
According to Jung, dreams can help us to get in touch with the "hidden gender" within us. The Anima is the

feminine part of a man's personality, and the Animus the masculine part of a woman's. Because society conditions us to behave in certain ways, we can easily lose touch with this vital part of ourselves; in our dreams, however, our inner selves are able to speak clearly. For male dreamers, any strong, sensible female character in a dream could represent your Anima, and the converse for female dreamers. Listen to what these figures have to say, and relate it to your waking life, and you may find yourself becoming better adjusted.

The Shadow

Jung suggested that we have deeply buried Shadow personalities, in many ways the opposite of the Personas that we consciously project in real life. The Shadow often gives us dreams that our conscious minds might be repelled by. For example, if in real life you are strongly disciplined, your Shadow might lean toward anarchy; if you are excessively neat and tidy in your everyday life, your Shadow might revel in extreme untidiness. Paying attention to what your Shadow says or does in your dreams can help you to become a more balanced individual.

Monsters

Your deepest fears or the least pleasant aspects of your personality might appear as a monster in your dreams. Next time you meet such a monster, try to take control of your dream: turn and face the monster, and ask it what it wants. This is a way of dealing safely with the dark side of yourself.

A RECORD OF YOUR DREAMS ABOUT RELIGION AND MYTHOLOGY

IMAGE	HOW IT APPEARED	DREAM NO. IN DIARY

PART TWO

YOUR DREAM DIARY

THE DREAM DIARY contains space for you to record sixty-five of your dreams, as well as your personal interpretations of them. You will find it helpful to consult the most common dream "themes" contained in the first part of this book. These themes will provide you with clues to the significance of your dreams. If you find your dreams difficult to remember, the advice given on the next page will help.

In addition to space to record your dreams, this section contains short entries that give you further information about dreams and their interpretations. The topics covered include information on how we dream, what dream analysts such as Freud and Jung had to say about dreams, and why their ideas are important. There are also entries on famous dreams in the Bible and in history, including some that might be warnings or prophecies. Dream folklore and evidence of waking dreams or visions are explored, as well as the phenomenon of people who "travel" in their dreams.

RECORDING YOUR DREAMS

WHENEVER YOU HAVE an interesting or disturbing dream, write it down in this dream diary. Doing this will enable you to analyze the dream and to record what you have learned about yourself. Over a period of time, this diary will provide a fascinating history of your dreams, and a valuable guide to your personality.

To ensure that you record every aspect of the dream, keep a notebook and a pen or pencil by your bed. The moment you wake from a dream, write it down in as much detail as you can; if you put this off until later, you are almost certain to forget most if not all of the dream. Use a rough notebook rather than this book to jot down your first impressions; your handwriting is unlikely to be at its best when you are still half asleep. You can write it up neatly later.

REMEMBERING THE DETAILS

The first few dreams that you record may be very sketchy because you have forgotten much of the detail, or you may have completely forgotten the ending by the time you have written the middle. Do not worry: the more you practice, the more detailed your entries will become.

Many people prefer to write down their dreams in chronological order, with each detail as it occurred. Others find it easier to jot down the important points first, then go back and fill in the background. Experiment with both methods to see which suits you best. When you have written down your dream, read it through. This will help

you to remember details you missed the first time. When you add more details, you may find a completely different version of the dream emerging, or perhaps that your first version was just a segment of a much larger dream. Sometimes this will prompt you to remember a link to an earlier dream that same night, or perhaps you will suddenly recall that you had a similar dream some days or weeks before. Make a note of these

occurrences (*see p. 29*). If certain aspects of the dream stand out as particularly significant, underline or highlight them because they may prove to be important. As you read through your dream and expand on your notes, you may find yourself beginning to interpret it right away; quite often this is when the meaning is the most clear. Write down your first impressions immediately. What was the mood of the dream? Think about how you felt within the dream – this is an important indicator of how the dream should be interpreted.

If you spend about ten minutes writing down your dream, it is probable that you will continue to remember it. If you just jot down a few words, then close your eyes and go back to sleep, you will probably be left with just a few unconnected words and no memory of how they should link together.

ANALYZING YOUR DREAM

Later, sit down with your rough notes, and with this book, and write down the important points of the dream in the diary section; include the mood, the setting, the story line, the characters, the colors – anything that strikes you as significant or unusual. Now consider the dream's main theme or the symbols that appeared. If the dream was about people, say, or was concerned with buildings, or indeed any theme in Part One, make a note of this in the diary, then turn to the relevant discussion about human life or buildings and structures in Part One and make a brief note there of your dream with its number.

Think about how this dream relates to your waking life. Do not be afraid to let your mind wander a little; sometimes the relevance of a dream is not immediately obvious. Let one thought trigger another; psychoanalysts call this free association, and it can be a very effective way to tease out the meaning of a dream. Write down in the diary your interpretation of the dream. Do not worry if this is very brief to begin with; as time goes by you will become more skilled at understanding your dreams.

LEARNING FROM YOUR DREAMS

From time to time, go back and read through all the dreams you have recorded here, and all the specific theme references in Part One. The storylines and details of the dreams may differ, but the same ideas may crop up over and over again. Ask yourself what your unconscious is telling you. Is it suggesting that you need to change in some way? If certain themes do recur, note whether there is any difference in them over time; if there is, this may indicate that you are succeeding in making any necessary changes in your life.

A RECORD OF YOUR RECURRING DREAMS

When you have a particular dream again and again, it can provide a useful insight to your unconscious: it is likely to be telling you about a problem that you need to deal with, such as a fear, a worry, or a lack of confidence in a certain area of your life. Although a recurrent dream can often be quite disturbing, by recording and analyzing it you can become familiar with it, understand what it is saying about you, and learn from it. The dream may not be exactly the same every time. The location or the outcome may alter: if, for example, you dream of running away from someone or something, you may get farther or less far on different occasions. The people in the dream may behave in different ways each time. The mood might also change. Take careful note of such differences, because they are likely to reflect the changes in your waking life as you begin to tackle the problem.

RECURRENT IMAGE	OBSERVATIONS	DREAM NO. IN DIARY

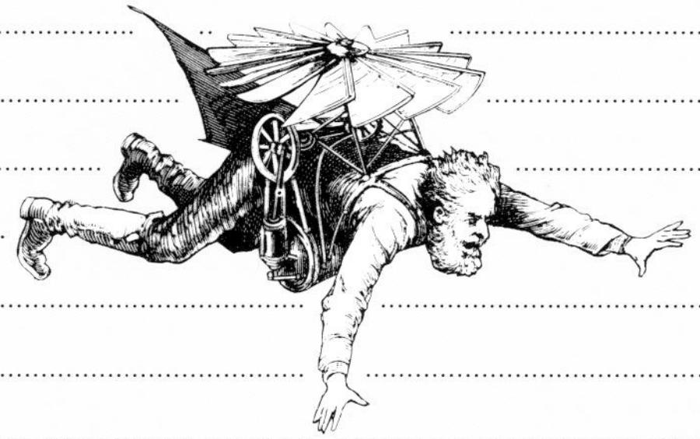

DREAM 1

YOUR DREAM

....
....
....
....
....
....
....
....
....
....
....

MOOD ....

COLORS ....

NUMBERS ....

OBJECTS ....

INTERPRETATION

....
....
....
....
....
....

DATE OF DREAM ....

DREAM 2

YOUR DREAM

....
....
....
....
....
....
....

MOOD ....

COLORS ....

NUMBERS ....

OBJECTS ....

INTERPRETATION

....
....
....
....

DATE OF DREAM ....

SLEEP AND DREAMS

Not only do we all dream, most of us have several dreams each night, even if we cannot recall them. Scientists can tell when sleepers are dreaming by monitoring their rapid eye movements (REM), brainwaves, and pulses. During normal sleep, we have four or five ninety-minute cycles, each encompassing four different levels of sleep. The levels of deep (dreamless) sleep last longer in the early stages of sleep but as the night goes on, the periods of light REM sleep (when we dream) get longer. This is why we often wake up out of a dream in the morning.

It is understood that sleep refreshes the body, but few people are aware that it is actually necessary to dream because dreams refresh the mind. Experiments in sleep deprivation have shown that it is probably not lack of sleep that disturbs people so much as dream deprivation. Yet we do not have any explanation of what dreams really are, nor why we have them. The most likely theory is that dreams are the result of the brain shuffling through its short-term memory of the day's events, storing some in the long-term memory, and discarding the rest.

Although some dreams seem to be no more than random images, many have coherent story lines. Dream analysts believe that in dreams our unconscious minds are helping us to understand ourselves, to solve our problems, and to provide us with clues that may allow us to improve our lives.

DREAM 3

YOUR DREAM

....

....

....

....

....

....

....

....

MOOD

....

      COLORS

....

      NUMBERS

....

OBJECTS

....

INTERPRETATION

....

....

....

....

....

DATE OF DREAM

DREAM 4

YOUR DREAM

....

....

....

....

....

....

....

....

MOOD

COLORS

NUMBERS

OBJECTS

INTERPRETATION

....

....

....

....

....

DATE OF DREAM

DREAM 5

YOUR DREAM

....

....

....

....

....

....

....

....

MOOD

COLORS

NUMBERS

OBJECTS

INTERPRETATION

....

....

....

....

....

DATE OF DREAM

DREAM 6

DREAM 7

YOUR DREAM

....
....
....
....
....
....
....
....
....
....
....
....
....

MOOD

COLORS

NUMBERS

OBJECTS

INTERPRETATION

....
....
....
....

DATE OF DREAM

YOUR DREAM

....
....
....
....
....
....
....
....
....

MOOD

COLORS

NUMBERS

OBJECTS

INTERPRETATION

....
....
....
....
....
....
....

DATE OF DREAM

SIGMUND FREUD

Sigmund Freud (1856–1939), known as the "father" of psychoanalysis, was the first in modern times to demonstrate that you can learn about yourself from your dreams. Freud's conclusion was that most dreams are about our hidden sexual fantasies and fears. He believed that our conscious minds are often repelled by our secret desires and that they repress these urges because we are ashamed of them, or are worried about how others might view us if they were known. Our unconscious minds, however, have full access to these hidden desires, and often draw attention to them in our dreams. It can be argued that Freud took this idea much too far; for him, everything in a dream became a symbol of some repressed urge (a fast car, a train in a tunnel, and even a pencil could, according to Freud, be a sexual symbol). Although Freud's terminology is still widely used, few analysts today follow his teachings uncritically. What is certain, though, is that our unconscious minds can be more honest than our conscious minds about our true characters – and it is this process of self-discovery that makes dream analysis such a fascinating, worthwhile, and revealing exercise.

DREAM 8

DREAM 9

DREAM 10

YOUR DREAM

YOUR DREAM

YOUR DREAM

MOOD

MOOD

MOOD

COLORS

COLORS

COLORS

NUMBERS

NUMBERS

NUMBERS

OBJECTS

OBJECTS

OBJECTS

INTERPRETATION

INTERPRETATION

INTERPRETATION

DATE OF DREAM

DATE OF DREAM

DATE OF DREAM

<table>
<tr><td>

DREAM 11

YOUR DREAM

....

....

....

....

....

....

....

....

....

</td><td>

MOOD

COLORS

NUMBERS

OBJECTS

INTERPRETATION

....

....

....

....

....

DATE OF DREAM

</td><td>

DREAM 12

YOUR DREAM

....

....

....

....

....

....

....

....

MOOD

COLORS

NUMBERS

OBJECTS

INTERPRETATION

....

....

....

....

....

....

DATE OF DREAM

</td></tr>
</table>

CARL JUNG

Carl Jung (1875–1961) began as a student of Freud (*see p. 32*) and later developed his own ideas about the meanings of dreams. His contributions to dream analysis are of great importance.

He conceived the concept of the Collective Unconscious, a great, shared pool of archetypal images that all people of all cultures draw from when they dream. Jung was not only a psychotherapist but also a philosopher and a scholar of mythology, among other things. He found that the same ideas occurred again and again in the myths of different cultures. This means that although some of your dream symbols may be specific to you, many of the symbols will be similar to those dreamed by other people.

Jung believed that dreams are much more than collections of symbols of repressed sexual desires. The contents of dreams, he concluded, including the storylines and the characters within them, are also important. Quite often these echo ancient myths; religious rituals, astrological symbols, and the old gods appear even in the dreams of people with no knowledge of or interest in religion or mythology.

Many of Jung's ideas have been incorporated into New Age philosophies and therapies, and are the background to some alternative religious movements.

34

DREAM 13

YOUR DREAM

....
....
....
....
....
....
....
....
....
....
....
....
....

MOOD ....
COLORS ....
NUMBERS ....
OBJECTS ....

INTERPRETATION

....

DATE OF DREAM ....

DREAM 14

YOUR DREAM

....
....
....
....
....
....
....
....
....
....
....
....
....

MOOD ....
COLORS ....
NUMBERS ....
OBJECTS ....

INTERPRETATION

....
....
....
....
....

DATE OF DREAM ....

DREAM 15

YOUR DREAM

....
....
....
....
....
....
....
....
....
....
....
....
....

MOOD ....
COLORS ....
NUMBERS ....
OBJECTS ....

INTERPRETATION

....
....
....
....
....
....
....

DATE OF DREAM ....

DREAM 16

YOUR DREAM

MOOD

COLORS

NUMBERS

OBJECTS

INTERPRETATION

DATE OF DREAM

DREAM 17

YOUR DREAM

"The dream, alone, is of interest. What is life without a dream?"

MOOD

COLORS

NUMBERS

OBJECTS

INTERPRETATION

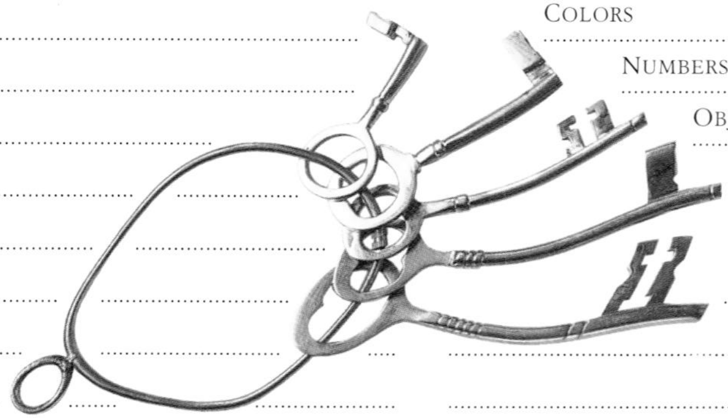

DATE OF DREAM

DREAM 18

YOUR DREAM

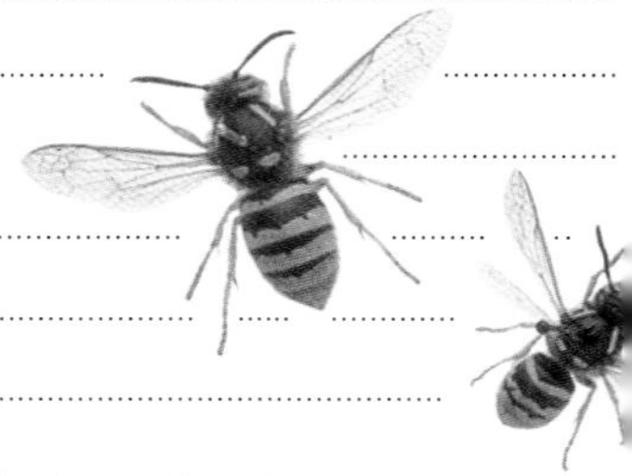

MOOD

COLORS

NUMBERS

OBJECTS

INTERPRETATION

DATE OF DREAM

DREAM 19

YOUR DREAM

....
....
....
....
....
....
....
....
....
....
....
....

MOOD ....

COLORS ....

NUMBERS ....

OBJECTS ....

INTERPRETATION

....
....
....
....
....
....

DATE OF DREAM ....

DREAM 20

YOUR DREAM

....
....
....
....
....
....
....
....
....
....
....
....
....
....

MOOD ....

COLORS ....

NUMBERS ....

OBJECTS ....

INTERPRETATION

....
....
....
....
....

DATE OF DREAM ....

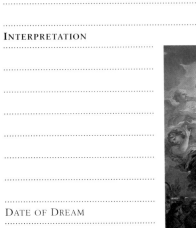

BIBLICAL DREAMS

The Bible contains evidence that people have been interpreting their dreams for thousands of years. The most famous Biblical dream is probably Pharaoh's dream about the seven fat and thin cattle, and the seven fat and thin ears of corn, which Joseph interpreted as a prophecy of seven years of plenty, followed by seven years of famine. Whether this dream was a warning from God or not, it does underscore the importance of noting down the numbers that appear in dreams (*see p. 46*). In Biblical times, people believed that

God sometimes spoke to them through their dreams. In the well-known Christmas story in Matthew's Gospel, "the angel of the Lord appeared to Joseph in a dream," warning him to flee to Egypt with the infant Jesus, to escape from King Herod.

Saint Peter had a vision or dream of animals and birds caught within a great sheet, and a voice telling him to kill and eat them. He protested that some of the creatures were "impure," not fit for a Jew to eat, and was told, "What God hath cleansed, that call thou not common" (Acts 10: 10-17). And when a number of Gentiles arrived at Saint Peter's house, he realized that his dream meant that he should welcome them and preach to them, for "God hath shewed me that I should not call any man common or unclean."

DREAM 21

YOUR DREAM

....

....

....

....

....

....

....

....

....

OBJECTS

....

INTERPRETATION

....

....

....

MOOD

COLORS

NUMBERS

DATE OF DREAM

DREAM 22

YOUR DREAM

....

....

....

....

....

....

....

MOOD

COLORS

NUMBERS

OBJECTS

INTERPRETATION

....

....

....

....

....

....

....

....

DATE OF DREAM

DREAMS THAT CHANGED HISTORY

Intangible and elusive as dreams are, they have been interpreted from the earliest times as powerful messages from the gods, inspiring people to act in ways that have altered the course of history. It is said that the Prophet Muhammad (AD 570–623) not only interpreted the dreams of his disciples, but also "received" much of the text of the Qur'an in a dream. Alexander the Great (356–323 BC) dreamed of a nature spirit, a satyr, dancing on his shield, and as a result attacked and conquered the city of Tyros. The French patriot Joan of Arc (1412–1431) believed that God instructed her through dream visions to save France from the English (*see p. 54*). Napoleon Bonaparte (1769–1821), emperor of France, saw entire military campaigns in his dreams, and on waking used toy soldiers to reenact them in a sandbox. Otto von Bismarck (1815–1898), chancellor of the German Empire, was guided by his dreams to implement policies that led to the establishment of Hitler's Fatherland. During World War II, it was a dream of being suffocated by falling debris that led Hitler to leave a bunker minutes before it was reduced to rubble by a shell, killing everyone inside.

DREAM 23

YOUR DREAM

MOOD

COLORS

NUMBERS

OBJECTS

INTERPRETATION

DATE OF DREAM

DREAM 24

YOUR DREAM

MOOD

COLORS

NUMBERS

OBJECTS

INTERPRETATION

DATE OF DREAM

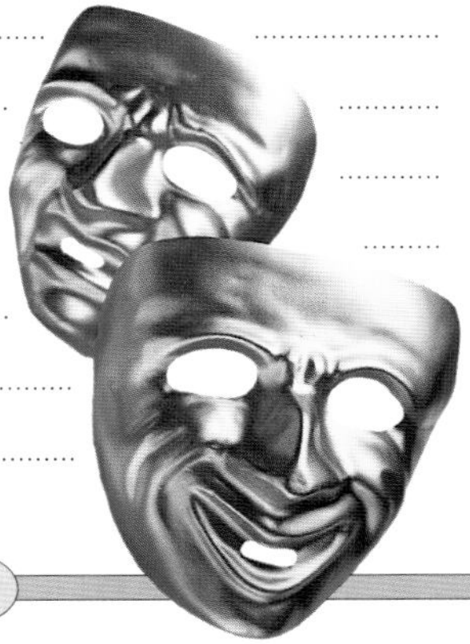

DREAM 25

YOUR DREAM

MOOD

COLORS

NUMBERS

OBJECTS

INTERPRETATION

DATE OF DREAM

DREAM 26

YOUR DREAM

....
....
....
....
....
....
....
....
....
....
....

MOOD ....
COLORS ....
NUMBERS ....
OBJECTS ....

INTERPRETATION

....
....
....
....
....
....
....

DATE OF DREAM ....

DREAM 27

YOUR DREAM

....
....
....
....
....
....
....
....
....
....
....

MOOD ....
COLORS ....
NUMBERS ....
OBJECTS ....

INTERPRETATION

....
....
....
....
....
....
....

DATE OF DREAM ....

WARNING DREAMS

Dreams can often contain images that we perceive as warnings about some future event in our lives. There are many stories of people who claim to have been "saved" by dreams. Dreaming of a plane crash the night before a flight is quite common, although few people go so far as to cancel their journeys. In nearly every case, the aircraft does not crash. If you have a similar dream, it probably means that your unconscious has taken in something about the trip that is worrying you, and has brought it to your attention in a dream.

Perhaps the most famous example of warning dreams that saved people's lives occurred when several passengers, having dreamed that the *Titanic* sank, decided at the last moment not to travel on the liner. One such dreamer was a London businessman, J. Connor Middleton, who dreamed of the ship being upside down, with people swimming around it. He cancelled his trip and lived to tell the tale. If you have a specific warning dream, for example of your car's brakes failing or its tires being blown out, it will do no harm to check your car. Your unconscious may have registered that something is amiss, and is letting you know; or at the very least your unconscious may be telling you that you are anxious about driving.

DREAM 28

YOUR DREAM

....
....
....
....
....
....
....
....

MOOD ....
COLORS ....
NUMBERS ....
OBJECTS ....

INTERPRETATION
....
....
....
....
....
....

DATE OF DREAM ....

DREAM 29

YOUR DREAM

....
....
....
....
....
....
....
....

MOOD ....
COLORS ....
NUMBERS ....
OBJECTS ....

INTERPRETATION
....
....
....
....
....
....

DATE OF DREAM ....

DREAM 30

YOUR DREAM

....
....
....
....
....
....
....
....

MOOD ....
COLORS ....
NUMBERS ....
OBJECTS ....

INTERPRETATION
....
....
....
....
....
....

DATE OF DREAM ....

DREAM 31

YOUR DREAM

....

....

....

....

....

....

....

....

....

....

....

....

....

MOOD ....

COLORS ....

NUMBERS ....

OBJECTS ....

INTERPRETATION

....

....

....

....

....

....

DATE OF DREAM ....

DREAM 32

YOUR DREAM

....

....

....

....

....

....

....

....

....

....

MOOD ....

COLORS ....

NUMBERS ....

OBJECTS ....

INTERPRETATION

....

....

....

....

....

....

....

....

DATE OF DREAM ....

PROPHETIC DREAMS

Of the countless numbers of dreams that are experienced every night all over the world, some are bound to come true, simply by the law of averages. And yet, is it merely a coincidence that several people dreamed that President Kennedy would be assassinated in the few days before it happened? Or are some people able to foresee the future in their dreams? If we could predict the future with any accuracy in our dreams, bookmakers would soon be out of business. Who could resist the temptation to bet on "a sure thing," whether it is a horse, a dog, a football game, or the lottery? One man who listened to his dreams in the 1940s was an English peer, Lord Kilbracken, who, after dreaming the winners of several horse races, placed successful bets, as did his friends.

Some people's dreams seem to be accurate so often that even the police are prepared to follow up their dream "tip-offs" in difficult cases. If you want to prove the validity of a prophetic dream – whether it is of an airplane crash, an assassination, a stock market collapse, or some other major event – you should write it down, date it, seal it, and give it to a trustworthy person before the event occurs.

DREAM 33

YOUR DREAM

MOOD

COLORS

NUMBERS

OBJECTS

INTERPRETATION

DATE OF DREAM

DREAM 34

YOUR DREAM

MOOD

COLORS

NUMBERS

OBJECTS

INTERPRETATION

DATE OF DREAM

DREAM 35

YOUR DREAM

MOOD

COLORS

NUMBERS

OBJECTS

INTERPRETATION

DATE OF DREAM

DREAM 36

YOUR DREAM

....

....

....

....

....

....

....

....

....

....

MOOD

COLORS

NUMBERS

OBJECTS

INTERPRETATION

....

....

....

....

....

....

DATE OF DREAM

DREAM 37

YOUR DREAM

....

....

....

....

....

....

MOOD

COLORS

NUMBERS

OBJECTS

INTERPRETATION

....

....

....

....

....

....

DATE OF DREAM

CREATIVE DREAMING

Many writers and artists have found inspiration for their work in their dreams. One of the most famous of these was the poet Samuel Taylor Coleridge, who woke from an opium dream about Kubla Khan with a long, descriptive poem fully formed in his head. Unfortunately, he was only part of the way through writing it down when he was interrupted by "a person from Porlock." This phrase has since passed into the English language; it means an unwelcome interruption, because by the time the visitor left, Coleridge had forgotten the rest of the poem, and it was never completed. Mary Shelley wrote *Frankenstein: or the Modern Prometheus* after she had had a particularly vivid dream. Some of the ideas in Robert Louis Stevenson's *Dr. Jekyll and Mr. Hyde* came from his disturbing dreams.

If you are artistic, try drawing or painting your dreams as well as writing them down. The colors, and often the mood and emotions of a dream, can be captured more easily in a visual form. To avoid suffering Coleridge's experience, you should start work as soon as you wake up – and stop for nothing.

DREAM 38

YOUR DREAM

....
....
....
....
....
....
....
....
....

MOOD ....
COLORS ....
NUMBERS ....
OBJECTS ....

INTERPRETATION

....
....
....
....
....

DATE OF DREAM ....

DREAM 39

YOUR DREAM

....
....
....
....
....
....
....
....
....

MOOD ....
COLORS ....
NUMBERS ....
OBJECTS ....

INTERPRETATION

....
....
....
....
....

DATE OF DREAM ....

DREAM 40

YOUR DREAM

....
....
....
....
....
....
....
....
....

MOOD ....
COLORS ....
NUMBERS ....
OBJECTS ....

INTERPRETATION

....
....
....
....
....

DATE OF DREAM ....

DREAM 41

YOUR DREAM

....

....

....

....

....

....

....

....

....

....

....

....

....

....

....

MOOD

....

COLORS

....

NUMBERS

....

OBJECTS

....

INTERPRETATION

....

....

....

....

....

....

....

DATE OF DREAM

....

DREAM 42

YOUR DREAM

....

....

....

....

....

....

....

....

....

....

....

....

....

....

MOOD

COLORS

NUMBERS

OBJECTS

INTERPRETATION

DATE OF DREAM

NUMBERS AND THEIR MEANINGS

Numbers that appear in dreams, whether as simple numerals or as a repeated number of objects, can be significant. The meanings of certain numbers may be relevant to you, such as a house number or a date, or they may be puns. Numbers also have old and deeply symbolic meanings, and whether or not we have studied mythology, religion, or philosophy, we can be aware of these meanings at an unconscious level.

0 Circle of the year, of reincarnation, nothingness.
1 Unity, one God, the individual, the male.
2 Pairs, opposites, balance, choice, the female.
3 The Christian Trinity, the Graces, the family; the progression of past, present, and future.
4 Matter, strength, solidity, the four elements, the seasons, the gospels.
5 Nature, the human being, esoteric spirituality.
6 Judaism (the Star of David), creation, sex.
7 Holiness, the seven colors of the rainbow, the Pillars of Wisdom, the Wonders of the World.
8 Practicality, infinity (when on its side), the Buddhist eight-fold Path of Wisdom.
9 Achievement, completion (as in pregnancy), Chinese and Buddhist spirituality.
10 The Commandments, the Hindu perfect number.
12 The Apostles, the signs of the Zodiac.

DREAM 43

YOUR DREAM

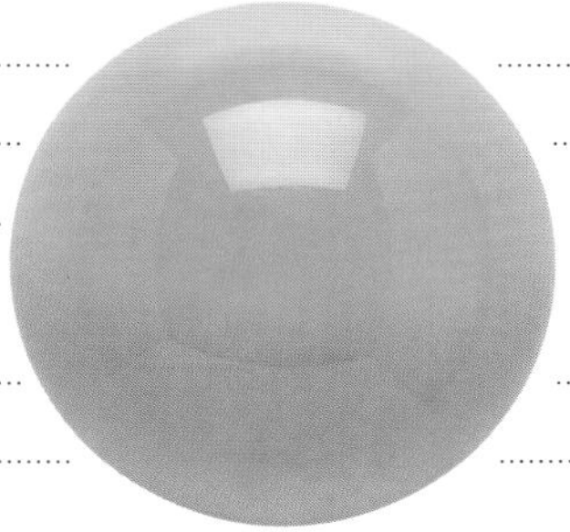

Mood

Colors

Numbers

Objects

INTERPRETATION

Date of Dream

DREAM 44

YOUR DREAM

Mood

Colors

Numbers

Objects

INTERPRETATION

Date of Dream

DREAM 45

YOUR DREAM

Mood

Colors

Numbers

Objects

INTERPRETATION

Date of Dream

DREAM 46

YOUR DREAM

MOOD

COLORS

NUMBERS

OBJECTS

INTERPRETATION

DATE OF DREAM

DREAM 47

YOUR DREAM

MOOD

COLORS

NUMBERS

OBJECTS

INTERPRETATION

DATE OF DREAM

DREAMS IN ART

For centuries, artists have been fascinated by sleep and dreams. When we are asleep we are physically vulnerable, and some paintings show this with great pathos, sometimes contrasting the defenseless sleeper with either a mortal or a supernatural guardian.

Occasionally dream-like paintings have a nightmarish quality, but more often they are romantic scenes, either of pastoral settings or of stylized classical beauty, as in the works of the Pre-Raphaelite artists. When romanticism and eroticism are portrayed in art it is usually with a dreamlike quality. In *There Sleeps Titania* (*see below*) by John Simmons (1823–1876), for example, the charm and beauty of an imagined fairy world is used to convey the blend of innocence and eroticism that is so characteristic of dreams.

While in our waking lives it is common to dismiss fantasy as unreal, such dreams can make full use of our imaginative powers. Our dreams are where our fantasies can come to life, and where impossible situations or images are acceptable. This happens in art as well; the paintings of surrealist artists such as Salvador Dali testify to this.

DREAM 48

YOUR DREAM

....
....
....
....
....
....
....
....
....
....

MOOD ....
COLORS ....
NUMBERS ....
OBJECTS ....

INTERPRETATION

....
....
....
....
....
....
....

DATE OF DREAM ....

DREAM 49

YOUR DREAM

....
....
....
....
....
....
....
....
....
....

MOOD ....
COLORS ....
NUMBERS ....
OBJECTS ....

INTERPRETATION

....
....
....
....
....
....
....

DATE OF DREAM ....

DREAM 50

YOUR DREAM

....
....
....
....
....
....
....
....
....
....

MOOD ....
COLORS ....
NUMBERS ....
OBJECTS ....

INTERPRETATION

....
....
....
....
....
....
....

DATE OF DREAM ....

DREAM 51

YOUR DREAM

....
....
....
....
....
....
....
....
....
....
....
....
....
....

MOOD ....

COLORS ....

NUMBERS ....

OBJECTS ....

INTERPRETATION

....
....
....
....
....
....
....
....

DATE OF DREAM ....

DREAM 52

YOUR DREAM

....
....
....
....
....
....
....
....
....
....
....
....
....
....

MOOD ....

COLORS ....

NUMBERS ....

OBJECTS ....

INTERPRETATION

....
....
....
....
....
....
....
....

DATE OF DREAM ....

DREAM TRAVEL AND MEETINGS

In primitive religions there are shaman figures, usually but not always male, who are able to travel in their dreams, or in drug-induced visions, into the spirit world. While there they ask the spirits of their ancestors, or the gods, for help, say in healing one of their people, or for answers to practical questions such as the best time to plant crops.

The Dreamtime of Australian aboriginal people is in some ways similar to Jung's theory of a Collective Unconscious (*see p. 34*). In their dreams, the aboriginals may still visit the shared place and time, the Alchera or Dreamtime, where the creator spirits walk and talk with humankind.

Some of today's esoteric religions postulate that in our dreams we may travel on different psychic planes and meet the "spirit bodies" of great teachers. Members of Theosophy and its offshoots, and of other religions such as the mystical Hindu/Sikh tradition, believe that they receive teaching from entities sometimes known as the Great White Brotherhood or the Hidden Masters.

Those people who are skilled at lucid dreaming claim that they are able to meet one another at an agreed place in their dreams.

DREAM 53

YOUR DREAM

MOOD

COLORS

NUMBERS

OBJECTS

INTERPRETATION

DATE OF DREAM

DREAM 54

YOUR DREAM

MOOD

COLORS

NUMBERS

OBJECTS

INTERPRETATION

DATE OF DREAM

DREAM 55

YOUR DREAM

MOOD

COLORS

NUMBERS

OBJECTS

INTERPRETATION

DATE OF DREAM

DREAM 56

YOUR DREAM

....
....
....
....
....
....
....

MOOD ....

COLORS ....

NUMBERS ....

OBJECTS ....

INTERPRETATION

....
....
....
....
....

DATE OF DREAM ....

DREAM 57

YOUR DREAM

....
....
....
....
....
....
....

MOOD ....

COLORS ....

NUMBERS ....

OBJECTS ....

INTERPRETATION

....
....
....
....
....

DATE OF DREAM ....

DREAM 58

YOUR DREAM

....
....
....
....
....
....
....

MOOD ....

COLORS ....

NUMBERS ....

OBJECTS ....

INTERPRETATION

....
....
....
....
....

DATE OF DREAM ....

"Friday nights dream on the Saturday told is sure to come true be it never so old."

DREAM 59

YOUR DREAM

....

....

....

....

....

....

....

....

....

....

....

....

MOOD

....

COLORS

....

NUMBERS

....

OBJECTS

....

INTERPRETATION

....

....

....

....

....

....

....

....

....

....

DATE OF DREAM

DREAM 60

YOUR DREAM

....

....

....

....

....

....

....

....

....

....

....

....

....

....

....

MOOD

COLORS

NUMBERS

OBJECTS

INTERPRETATION

....

....

....

....

....

....

....

DATE OF DREAM

DREAM FOLKLORE

Dreams have always been surrounded by superstition and folklore. At one time it was believed that dreams always meant the opposite of what they were about: if you dreamed of poverty it meant that you would become wealthy, and vice versa. This rule of opposites was very convenient for any religious devotee who had erotic dreams, because it must obviously have meant that he or she was pure in thought.

There has always been a strong popular belief that dreams can foretell the future. Only a century ago, if a girl wanted to know the name of her future husband she would make a cake on St. Agnes's Eve, mark her initials on the top, and bake it overnight. She would then dream of her suitor.

In *The Duchess of Malfi* by John Webster (1580–1625), the duchess says of dreaming about pearls, "You'll weepe shortly . . . the pearles doe signify your teares". Another old belief was that "to dream of coals is a sign of riches." Few people believe this now, but other superstitions linger on. Some still believe, for example, that eating cheese before going to bed gives you nightmares. The belief persists, although we know rationally that our sleep patterns and dream levels will be disturbed if we eat, last thing at night, any food that is difficult to digest.

XV

LE·DIABLE

DREAM 61

YOUR DREAM

....
....
....
....
....
....
....
....
....
....
....
....

MOOD ....

COLORS ....

NUMBERS ....

OBJECTS ....

INTERPRETATION

....
....
....
....
....
....

DATE OF DREAM ....

DREAM 62

YOUR DREAM

....
....
....
....
....
....
....
....
....
....
....
....

MOOD ....

COLORS ....

NUMBERS ....

OBJECTS ....

INTERPRETATION

....
....
....
....
....
....
....

DATE OF DREAM ....

VISIONS

A vision is a kind of waking dream. It can happen to anyone, not just to religious mystics, but also to the psychologically disturbed or those under the influence of drugs. A vision can be a momentary flash of an image, but sometimes it lasts longer and seems to contain clear messages. It used to be commonly believed – and still is by some – that visions were messages from God.

In the 15th century a young French girl, later known as Joan of Arc (*see p. 38*), saw visions in which saints told her to help the Dauphin of France in his battles. She obeyed, and fought alongside the Dauphin, but although she was with him when he was crowned Charles VII, she was later captured, sold to the English, and burned at the stake as a witch. She was canonized in 1920.

Many religious mystics, as well as some ordinary people, have seen visions, often of the glory of God. The well-known prophecies of Nostradamus were originally seen in visions, and places where visions have occurred, such as Lourdes and Fatima, have become famous pilgrimage sites.

DREAM 63

YOUR DREAM

....
....
....
....
....
....
....
....
....
....
....

MOOD ....
COLORS ....
NUMBERS ....
OBJECTS ....

INTERPRETATION

....
....
....
....
....
....
....

DATE OF DREAM ....

DREAM 64

YOUR DREAM

....
....
....
....
....
....
....
....
....
....
....

MOOD ....
COLORS ....
NUMBERS ....
OBJECTS ....

INTERPRETATION

....
....
....
....
....
....
....

DATE OF DREAM ....

DREAM 65

YOUR DREAM

....
....
....
....
....
....
....
....
....
....
....

MOOD ....
COLORS ....
NUMBERS ....
OBJECTS ....

INTERPRETATION

....
....
....
....
....
....
....

DATE OF DREAM ....

ACKNOWLEDGMENTS

PICTURE CREDITS

a=above; b=bottom; bg=background; c=center; l=left; r=right; t=top

Ashmolean Museum: 34cla, 34cr; **Bridgeman Art Library:** Belvoir Castle, Leicestershire, *Three Graces* by Antonio Canova (1757–1822) (marble) 46cl; Prado, Madrid, *Solomon's Dream* by Luca Giordano (1632–1705) 37b; Private Collection, *There Sleeps Titania*, 1872 by John Simmons (1823–76) 48br; Private Collection, *The Titanic Sinking on 15th April 1912*, 1991 by Harley Crossley 40cr; **British Museum:** 24cl, 27bl, 53tr; **Camera Press:** Karsh of Ottawa 34bl; **ET Archive:** 38cl; **Mary Evans Picture Library:** 53br, 54cr; Max Halberstadt/© Freud 32bl; **Ronald Grant Archive:** *Bride of Frankenstein* © Universal 44bl; **Robert Harding Picture Library:** 39bc; **Image Bank:** 4cra; Paul Biddle 48bl; D. Carroll 38bl; Will Crocker 9cr, 28c; Michael Dunning 51cl; Tracy Frankel 12tr; Steve Krongard 49bc; John Martin 16cra; Steve Mcalister 43cr; Andre Plessel 30bc; Elle Schuster 22tr, 29bl, 32cla, 35bl, 37cra, 55br; M. Tcherevkoff 7br, 13br, 22cl, 38/39c; Pete Turner 6/7bg, 20bl, 26/27bg; Andy Zito 51cr; **Images Colour Library:** 1bg, endpapers, 8br, 10ca, 10/11bg, 16cl, 23cr, 38tc, 39c; **Imperial War Museum:** 11tl; **National Maritime Museum:** 1cl, 5cla, 12bl, 45bl, 50tc; **Press Association/Topham:** 42bl; **Science Museum:** 2tc, 13tc; **Tony Stone Images:** James Darell 11cl; Philip Habib 20cra; Richard Johnston 16/17bg; **Superstock Ltd:** 22tl, 23t, 23br.

Jacket: **British Museum:** front tc, back tc; **Robert Harding Picture Library:** front tr, back tr; **National Maritime Museum:** front br.

QUOTATION SOURCES

Page 9 Ralph Waldo Emerson (1803–1882)
Page 13 John Bunyan (1628–1688), *Pilgrim's Progress*
Page 15 Tertullian (*c*.160–*c*.220)
Page 17 Above: William Shakespeare (1564–1616), *Hamlet;*
Page 17 Below: Daniel Defoe (?1661–1731)
Page 19 Alfred, Lord Tennyson (1809–1892), *Locksley Hall*
Page 31 Alfred, Lord Tennyson (1809–1892), *The Higher Pantheism*
Page 33 William Shakespeare (1564–1616), *The Tempest*
Page 35 John Keats (1795–1821), *Lamia*
Page 36 Edmond Rostand (1868–1918), *La Princesse Lointaine*
Page 38 Edgar Allan Poe (1809–1849), *The Raven*
Page 41 W. B.Yeats (1865–1939), *He Wishes For the Cloths of Heaven*
Page 42 Logan Pearsall Smith (1865–1946)
Page 45 Chuang-Tzu (*c*.350 BC)
Page 47 Robert Herrick (1591–1674), *A Country Life: to his Brother, M.Tho. Herrick*
Page 49 Michel de Montaigne (1533–1592)
Page 51 Anton Chekhov (1868–1904), *The Seagull*
Page 52 Old English proverb
Page 53 Old Irish saying
Page 55 Rabin-Dranath Tagore (1861–1941), *Fireflies*